# CURRENCIES OF THE WORLD

## HOW MONEY WORKS

# CURRENCIES OF THE WORLD

# HOW MONEY WORKS

Julie Ellis

young
reed

# CONTENTS

# INTRODUCTION

How much money have you got in your piggy bank? Are you saving up for something special?

Have you ever used an automatic teller machine? Have you ever been given a cheque? Can you earn money from doing chores, or helping your neighbours in their garden?

This book is all about money. It takes you from the earliest times, when people traded food and tools, to modern-day Internet banking.

The contents page gives you an overview of the topics covered in this book, and the pages you will find them.

Each double page spread discusses one topic. You don't have to start at the beginning of the book. You can read the pages in any order.

The words printed in bold type have their meanings explained in the Glossary on page 46.

There is an index on page 48.

If you want to find out more about currency, try the list of websites on page 47.

If you are interested in art, geography, history, earning money, or even magic tricks, this book has information for you.

So what are you waiting for? Open it up and start reading.

# Let's TRADE

## Early trading

Thousands of years ago, groups of people moved around hunting and gathering their food. When two groups met they would swap things with each other. They might swap some sharp hard rocks for some fish, or animal skins for spears. Swapping one thing for another is also called **trading**. Years later, when tribal groups met explorers, they also traded with the explorers.

Pieces of flint were used as trade items

## Swapping skills

Some groups of people stopped being hunters; it was easier to stay in one place and farm animals for food. They could also grow crops if they stayed in one place. Not everyone needed to produce food. Some people developed other skills such as pottery, or weaving. The craftspeople needed food, so they traded their goods with the people who grew the crops. Trading without using money is known as **barter**.

A modern craftsperson weaves on a loom

## Ancient Egyptian businesspeople

The ancient Egyptians developed a complex bartering system. Not only did they barter for goods and services amongst themselves, they also managed to barter with foreign countries.

The Egyptians exported grain, linen and papyrus in exchange for timber from Lebanon, copper from Cyprus and incense from Afghanistan.

The ancient Egyptians obtained many goods through barter, as seen in The Tomb of Nakht

6

## Double trading

You are a fisherman and you want to trade some of your fish for a new pot. The potter doesn't want your fish; he wants a rug. You have to trade your fish with the weaver to get a rug, then you can trade the rug with the potter. **Double trading** is very complicated. You have to trade quickly in case someone changes his mind about trading with you, or trades with someone else. You also have to trade quickly before your fish rots.

## How many chickens for a goat?

People often couldn't agree on what things were worth. How many apples equalled one goat? How many fish equalled one clay pot? What was one chicken worth? Bartering got so difficult that people thought of a different way to trade. They needed an item with an agreed symbolic value. Then anything could be exchanged for the symbolic item.

This goat is valuable to this boy because he can keep it and have milk to drink, or he can trade it for something else he needs, but what is his goat worth? How many apples, chickens or pots could he get for his goat?

## Symbolic value

Using an item with a **symbolic value** is useful for many reasons.
1. You can agree on a price.
2. It is easy to transport. You don't have to carry heavy items around with you.
3. It is easy to store because it doesn't take up much space.
4. It is easy to divide (it's tricky to trade half a goat with someone!).
5. It can be saved until you need to spend it, without losing value (fruit and vegetables quickly go rotten, so they need to be traded while they are fresh).
6. It doesn't need to be cared for (goats need food, water and shelter).
7. It is accepted for all goods and services so you don't have to double trade to get what you want.

# Rats, beans &

## Supply and demand

When something is difficult to supply it becomes valuable. When something is easy to supply it is not valuable. This is called the law of **supply and demand**. Items that are valuable in a culture become its money or currency. Different cultures value different items. A small island culture that lacks meat would value rats highly. Rats are easy to look after as they don't require much food or space, and they are a valuable source of meat. In other countries, where rats are plentiful, they would not be viewed as valuable.

## Worth your salt

We all need salt in our diet or we get very sick. Salt is also needed for preserving meats in hot climates. In ancient times, salt was hard to find and collect, so it became very valuable.

The word 'salary' comes from the Latin word *salarium*, meaning 'salt money'. Early Roman soldiers were paid in salt. Based on this, there is a saying that a person is 'worth their salt', meaning they were worth the money they were paid.

## What can be used as money?

The ancient Mayans and Aztecs used cacao beans as currency. They were used in all kinds of ways: in food and drink, as a medicine and at religious ceremonies. Cacao beans look like grey pebbles, or dirty almonds. They don't look valuable. Unfortunately, when English explorers captured a boatload of cacao beans they didn't realise the beans were valuable and they sank the cargo.

Yap's stone money bank

## Heavy money

The world's heaviest money is found on the island of Yap, in Micronesia. These huge stones (taller than a man) were valuable because they were difficult to get. Yapese warriors had to sail 200 miles to quarry the stones, and then they had to bring them back to Yap.

The coins are still used as legal tender on the island. Even though ownership of the coins may change, the coins are not shifted. Most of the stone money is stored in a canal known as the money bank.

## Shells

Many cultures used shells as money. They could be made into ornaments and were easy to carry, store and count. The type of shell used as currency was one that was rare to that culture.

Some Native Americans used wampum (small cut shells that are strung together). In northern Australia, different tribes used different shells, with one tribe's shell often being quite worthless in the eyes of another tribe. The ancient Chinese and Indians both used cowrie shells.

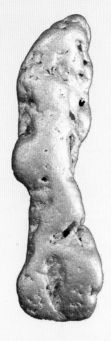

## Precious metals

Some currencies didn't work well as money. Animals were hard to transport, fish would go rotten and shells could break. People needed a currency that was easy to carry, would not break, and was rare and therefore valuable. Gradually, precious metals such as gold, silver, **electrum** and copper became the main currencies. They could be used to make ornaments and weapons, but they were also rare. Because precious metals were so useful, they were easy to trade with anyone. People could say how much gold or silver their goods or services were worth. The value of a piece of metal depended on its weight, not its size or shape.

# Old MONEY

## The first coins

Weighing metal was a slow way to trade. In about 600 BCE the people in Lydia worked out a better way to exchange precious metals. They melted metal and shaped it into tiny discs. Each disc was stamped with a picture according to its weight. The picture told people the weight and value of each disc. Because counting was quicker and easier than weighing, the use of these discs spread rapidly to other countries.

In Greece, each city made its own coins. Coins from important cities like Athens and Corinth were known by their images. Coins from Athens were called owls, and the coins of Corinth were called foals. They were used internationally because everyone recognised them, and trusted their value.

Early Athenian coins

## Coins in China

Originally, coins in China had holes in their centres so they could be threaded on a string and worn around the neck instead of being carried in a purse.

## Coins today

Today, the **Mint** produces coins in each country. They are made from non-precious metals such as copper, nickel and zinc. Coins are worth more than the metal they are made from. The government that issues a coin decides what that coin is worth.

Ancient China

# Banknotes as receipts

Goldsmiths used to look after wealthy people's gold for them. The goldsmith would give the owner a handwritten receipt, which promised to pay the person back on demand. This was called a **running cash note**. Sometimes the goldsmith would pay the gold to whoever gave him back the receipt. This meant the receipt could be passed around from one person to another, like a modern banknote.

# Banknotes as currency

The Bank of England was established in 1694. It issued notes for the money left in its care (**deposits**). Banknotes became popular because carrying large amounts of coins was a nuisance. The bank was allowed to issue paper money even if there wasn't actually the same amount of gold in the bank. Banknotes were no longer receipts to be exchanged for gold. They were notes that were valuable because the bank promised to pay the bearer the value printed on the note.

# Paper money

The earliest use of paper money was in China more than 1000 years ago. Merchants could exchange heavy coins for light paper receipts, issued by shopkeepers. The notes could only be used locally, so the use of paper money did not become widespread. In the 11th century, Bi Sheng invented a movable type printer. This meant it was easier to print standardised money. Within two centuries the Chinese government had produced a nationwide currency.

Goldsmiths at work

# MAKING money

## Planning a coin

Coins are made at **Mints**. Coins must be tough, light, easy to distinguish from each other and hard to copy. There are many decisions to be made when a new coin is made. What size, weight, colour and shape will the coin be? What value will it have, and what will the design look like?

Artist making large cast of coin

## Designing a coin

First, an artist makes a large drawing of the design on both sides of the new coin. Then large casts of both the obverse and the reverse drawings are made. An engraving machine then carves tiny metal copies of the casts. The metal copies are called dies. The dies are put in the coining press.

Sheets of metal after coins have been cut out

## Cutting and pressing coins

All coins start as **blanks**, which are round pieces of metal, punched out of metal sheets.

The blanks are heated, washed and dried. Then they go in a rimming machine, which makes rims around the edge of each blank. If you run your fingers around a coin, you can feel the bumpy rim. Next the blanks go into the coining press, where the dies stamp each blank with its obverse and reverse design at the same time. The blank is now a coin. All the coins are checked, counted and bagged, ready to be sent to the banks.

New coins on a conveyor belt

# Can my picture go on a banknote?

Banknotes are printed at banknote printers. Like coins, banknotes must be tough, light, easy to distinguish from each other and hard to copy. Some countries make their banknotes from **polymer**, a kind of plastic, and other countries use tough paper. The **Reserve Bank** decides which people will feature on a currency note. The public can make suggestions, but the people chosen must be important to their country.

Sir Apirana Ngata appears on the New Zealand $50.00 note. He was a prominent Maori politician.

## The banknote is designed

Each banknote design includes an important symbol, a portrait of someone famous, and words that show the value and the country of issue. Once a design is chosen, an artist makes large drawings. The drawings are used to create several different printing plates. The printing plates are put into several different printing machines. Each machine prints only part of the banknote.

## The banknote is printed

Large sheets of polymer or notepaper are put through a series of printing machines. Dozens of banknotes are printed on one sheet. Each machine prints one part of the final design. Part of each note has a raised print, called **intaglio**, which you can feel with your fingers. When all parts of the design have been printed **serial numbers** are added. The sheets of banknotes are cut into individual banknotes. The banknotes are counted and wrapped, ready to be sent to the banks.

Uncut sheets of US$2 bills.

# How to become a
# NUMISMATIST

## How do you say that?

Numismatics (NEW-mis-MAT-ics) is the study of money. A numismatist (new-MIS-ma-TIST) is someone who collects and studies money. In some countries shells were used as money, so a numismatist might collect money shells. Coin collecting became a trend in the 14th century. In those days only wealthy people could afford to collect coins, so it became known as 'The Hobby of Kings'. Nowadays anyone can become a coin collector.

## Your collection

You should collect what interests you the most. A coin doesn't have to be valuable or rare to be collected. Something common is easier to find and cheaper to buy. You can arrange your coins in any way you like. You might group them according to shape, size, value, or countries you have visited. You could also group them according to their artwork (e.g. coins featuring animals), or what they are made from (e.g. copper).

Unusual-shaped coins

## Heads or tails?

Have you ever played the 'heads or tails' coin-flipping game? Traditionally, every coin had a head side and a tail side. However, some of the new Euro coins don't have a head on them. So how can we tell which is the head (or obverse) side? The obverse side of a Euro has the date and a symbol of the country that minted it. The reverse side of the Euro states the coin's value. When coins don't have a head on them, the side that bears the name of the country is usually considered the obverse.

Euro coins obverse and reverse

# Parts of a coin

**Field:** The blank area of a coin that has no design or words.

**Legend:** The main words on a coin.

**Mint mark:** In the United States there are six coin mints. Each mint stamps the coins with a different small letter identifying which mint struck the coin, e.g. D for Denver.

**Edge:** The outer border of a coin, considered the 'third side' (not the same as the 'rim').

**Rim:** The raised edge on both sides of a coin that helps protect the coin's design from wear.

**Relief:** The part of a coin's design that is raised above the surface.

## Storing your collection

It is important to handle your coin collection with care. Coins that are scratched, rubbed or polished lose collector value. You need a magnifying glass and plastic tweezers so that you can look at your coins closely without touching them. If you touch your coins too often, the grease from your hands will damage them. Clean coins may look nice but they are worth less, because they are likely to have been damaged during cleaning. Store your coins in proper storage containers where they won't bump against each other.

A US silver dollar collection

## Rare coins

There are rare coins in all countries. The rarest coin in Australia is the 1930 penny: only six of these pennies are known to exist. There are several coins that could be considered the rarest coin in the United States. Those coins where only one is known to exist include the 1851 Seated Liberty Dollar, and the 1870 $3 old Piece. A rare British coin is the 1817 *The Three Graces* crown. The three figures on the reverse side of the coin represent Ireland, Britain and Scotland.

# Finding FORGERIES

## A work of art

Have you ever looked at a banknote with a magnifying glass? You will see fine line patterns and tiny details. If you hold a note to the light you can see even more features. There are two reasons why banknotes are such works of art. Firstly, they are designed by talented artists. Secondly, the fine details and security features make it harder for people to forge notes.

## Collecting banknotes

Notaphily (noh-TAF-uh-lee) is the study of banknotes. A notaphilist (noh-TAF-uh-list) is a collector of bank notes, paper money, or plastic notes. Banknote collecting is becoming a popular hobby because it is easy to find interesting bank notes. There are banknotes from countries that no longer exist, and from newly formed countries. You can collect notes according to country, value, picture, serial number or even the year you were born. Some people even collect **forgeries** (fake money), which have no value but are interesting.

A banknote from Yugoslavia, a country that no longer exists.

## Operation Bernhard

Operation Bernhard was the codename of a secret Nazi plan during World War II to destabilise the British economy by dropping thousands of forged £5, £10, £20 and £50 notes from planes into Britain. The Nazis hoped British people would spend the money, causing **inflation** in Britain.

However, the Nazis didn't have enough planes, so they gave the **counterfeit** money to their spies instead. The Bank of England declared the forgeries 'the most dangerous ever seen'. They looked so real, the Bank of England had to withdraw all notes larger than £5 from circulation. They did not start reintroducing other denominations until the 1960s.

# Security features on a US$ 20

1. The special paper and ink used give a distinctive texture and appearance to the banknote.
2. The watermark to the right of the portrait shows the same figure as the portrait, but can only be seen when held up to a light.
3. A security thread embedded to the left of the portrait glows green in ultraviolet light. The words 'USA TWENTY' and a flag are printed on the thread.
4. Colour-shifting ink in the numeral on the lower right corner reflects in the light.

# Security features on an AU$ 10

1. The note is made from polymer.
2. A clear window with a windmill and an embossed wave pattern printed on it can be seen on both sides of the note.
3. When the note is held up to the light, a seven-pointed star within a circle is visible.
4. A shadow image of the Australian Coat of Arms can be seen when the note is held to the light.
5. Intaglio is used for the portrait of 'Banjo' Paterson, the word 'Australia' and the numeral '10'.
6. Excerpts from the poem 'The Man from Snowy River' are micro printed in the area surrounding 'Banjo' Paterson's portrait and can be seen with a magnifying glass.

# How to spot a forgery

1. Get to know the currency of your country. Are your notes paper or polymer? What do the various issues of the notes look like? What security features does your country use?
2. Feel the note. Real banknotes have raised print called **intaglio,** which you can feel.
3. Hold it up to the light. All notes have some visual security features such as a **watermark**, a clear window with **embossing**, a **shadow image**, colour-shifting ink (changes colour in the light), a **security thread** and **serial numbers**.
4. Look at the details. Real notes have clear, sharp details. Forgeries tend to be blurred.
5. Compare the note to another bill of the same value. Are they identical? If your note has even one difference, it is probably a forgery.

# As safe as the
# BANK OF ENGLAND

## A safe place

Banks were originally safe places for wealthy people to deposit their gold. In ancient times, temples were the safest places because no one would steal from a temple, People believed that if they stole from a temple the gods would be angry with them.

Al Khazneh is a building in the ancient city of Petra in Jordan. It was carved out of a sandstone rock face in 100 BCE. No one knows what it was used for, but its name means 'The Treasury' in Arabic.

Al Khazneh in Petra, Jordan

Safe deposit boxes in a bank

## Money in

Most adults today keep their money in a bank. It's much safer than keeping it at home. This is called depositing money. We can also deposit other valuables at a bank. Many banks allow you to store important papers or jewellery in a safe deposit box. All the safe deposit boxes are kept in a room called a vault. Each box is locked. You keep the key for your safe deposit box.

## How interesting

Many people deposit their money into the same bank. That bank now has lots of money. It lends out some of this money to people who need a loan. The bank charges interest on the money it lends out. The bank gives some of the interest to the people who deposited their money. It keeps the rest of the interest to pay the bank staff and for other costs.

## Commercial banks

Banks that provide services to people, such as accepting deposits and making loans, are called commercial banks. These banks also provide other banking services. They issue **cheque books** and **credit cards**. They provide automatic teller machines (ATMs) so that people can deposit and withdraw money when the bank is closed. Commercial banks also send account statements to their customers, and can ensure regular bills are paid automatically from customers' accounts.

Using an Automatic Teller Machine (ATM)

The Bank of England

## Central banks

You can't deposit money at the central bank, but your bank can. In each country there is one central bank that is owned by the government. The central bank controls the commercial banks. It sets the value of your country's currency against other world currencies. This is called the OCR (official cash rate). Central banks are the only banks allowed to print money.

Some well-known central banks include the Australian Reserve Bank, the 12 Federal Reserve Banks in the USA, the European Central Bank and the Bank of England. Because it has been at Threadneedle Street since 1734, the Bank of England is known as 'The Old Lady of Threadneedle Street.' It is well guarded, giving rise to the phrase 'as safe as the Bank of England'.

## Dollars and sense

It makes sense to keep your money in a bank. Whether you want a new mobile phone, a car, or a college education, you will achieve your goal quicker if you deposit your money in a savings account. You can set savings targets, watch your money grow and receive interest on your money. The bank will send you regular statements showing how much you have deposited, how much interest the bank has paid you, and whether you have been charged any bank fees.

Bank deposit book

# A world
# FREE OF POVERTY

## The World Bank

The World Bank is different from all other banks. You can't make a deposit or withdrawal from this bank and you can't ask for a loan. The World Bank was set up to loan money, not to individuals, but to countries. The loans improve the lives of billions of people throughout the world, many of them children.

The World Bank slogan is 'Working for a world free of poverty'.

## Who owns the World Bank?

The World Bank is owned by 184 different countries, and they all give money to the bank. The bank also invests and borrows money. The money is used for many large projects, including improving education, health and living conditions. In 2007 the bank loaned more than US$24 billion for more than 300 projects worldwide.

## The cost of living

How much does it cost to keep your family alive for one day? Food, clothing, shelter, education, health and electricity cost a lot of money. According to the World Bank, 1.4 billion people earn $1.25 or less a day. They live in extreme poverty. They can't afford electricity. In Bolivia, the World Bank is helping with the cost of providing 15,000 houses with solar panels for electricity.

Houses in Bolivia

**184 banks put money into**

**The World Bank**

**EDUCATION
HEALTH
LIVING CONDITIONS**

# Free education

Imagine if you couldn't go to school, because you had to work and earn money, or because there was no school near where you lived. In some countries children are unable to go to school. A major World Bank goal is to ensure that all children throughout the world receive free primary school education by 2015.

# Nothing to eat

Have you ever felt hungry? The less food there is, the more it costs. In some countries children starve because there is not enough food, or it costs too much.

One World Bank project is the Emergency Food Project for Niger. A grant from the World Bank is helping pay the cost of fertiliser for rice. This is important because it means more rice can be grown quickly, so the people won't starve.

# Keeping healthy

Have you ever been sick? Children in poor countries often get sick. One serious illness in Africa is called malaria. Children get malaria from mosquito bites. The World Bank is giving money to control malaria. Some of the money is being used to make bed nets. The nets stop mosquitoes from biting children, so the children don't get sick.

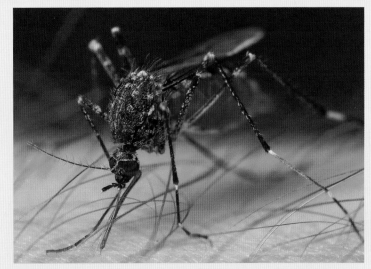

Children in Africa are at risk of getting malaria from mosquitoes

# BALANCING *act*

## The economy

The economy is the balance between the goods and services people want, and what is being produced. You are a part of many economies, including local, national and global economies.

The local economy is managed by your local council. It must balance local needs such as a public library, street lighting and rubbish collection, with the money it receives in rates (council taxes).

A rubbish collection service

## A balanced world

Many countries throughout the world are connected through trade. Trade between different countries creates a global economy. It is important that the global economy is kept in balance. The G-20 is a group of finance ministers and bank governors from different countries. In 2009 the G-20 met in London. They discussed ways to balance world trade so that all countries would benefit.

## Balancing the budget

The national economy is managed by the government. It has to balance supplying education, health care, defence and other needs with the amount of tax it has collected. In many countries the **Treasury** produces a yearly spending plan known as 'the budget'. It shows how the government plans to raise funds and spend money in the upcoming year. The amount of money governments spend can be huge. In 2008 the United States federal budget allocated spending of US$2.98 trillion.

# How taxing

Everyone who earns money must pay part of their earnings to their government. This is called taxation. The money from tax is used to pay for things everyone needs such as roads, hospitals and schools.

There is also a goods and services tax (GST) or value added tax (VAT) in most countries. Whenever you buy something or pay for someone to provide a service, some of the money goes to the government as tax.

# A mixed economy

Most countries have a mixed economy. This means that some goods and services are provided by the government, and some goods and services are provided by people who want to make money. A mixed economy gives everyone more choice. For example, parents can choose to send their children to state schools or to private schools. If you had the choice, would you prefer to go to a private school, which has a wider range of subjects, but costs money, or a state school, which is free but might not offer as many subjects?

Studying science at school

# Mini economy

These two boys have set up a business. They had to supply lemons, sugar, glasses, a jug, wood and paint for their sign. They also supplied labour and time. What price should they sell their lemonade for? They might have to adjust

A small business

their price according to supply and demand. What if it is a hot day, or a cold day? What time of day would there be the most customers? How would the competition of another lemonade stand affect their business? Should the boys share the profits 50/50? These boys have to consider many variables to ensure they balance **expenditure** against **income**, and make a **profit**.

# How do you want
# TO PAY?

## Ways to pay

Coins and banknotes are not the only ways to pay people. Cheque books have been a very popular method of payment. A cheque is safer than cash because only the person the cheque is made out to can bank it. If it is lost or stolen, no one else can bank it. However, advances in electronic banking mean credit cards, debit cards and Internet banking are becoming more common methods of payment.

Paying with cash

Paying with a cheque

## Goodbye to cheque books?

The Payments Council (a group of bankers) in Britain is pushing for cheques to be abolished by 2018 because it claims they are more expensive to process than electronic payments, and fewer people are using them. However, because many older people use cheques rather than electronic transfers, groups such as Age Concern are opposing the move to get rid of cheques.

## Put it on credit

If you have a **credit card**, you can buy something before you have the money to pay for it. The bank will let you do this because you then have to repay the money for the item you bought and pay the bank interest for using their money. The bank makes money from the **interest** they charge you. Credit cards have security features such as your photo, your signature, a hologram and a card expiry date.

# Debit cards

If you have a savings account, you can get a **debit card**. Each time you use a debit card, money is debited from your account. If there is no money in your account, your debit card will be rejected. Your debit card has a PIN (personal identification number). If you lose your card no one else can access your money because they don't know your PIN.

Buying groceries with a debit card

A husband and wife pay bills online

# Internet banking

Internet banking means you pay your bills online. You can pay your bills from the comfort of your own home, at a time that suits you (even if your bank is shut). As well as paying your bills, you can access your account information and transfer money from one account to another. It is safe as long as you have good antitheft software on your computer.

# Hire purchase

If someone wants to buy a car and they don't have enough money, what can they do? They can buy it on hire purchase. This means the buyer pays a deposit of as much money as they can, and then the rest of the money owing can be paid through a series of monthly instalments. However, these monthly payments include interest. The seller receives more than they would get if they sold the car in one transaction, but they have to wait longer for their money. The buyer gets the item they want immediately, but they end up having to pay more money for it.

Buying a new car on hire purchase

# A bull or a BEAR?

Stockbrokers

## What is the stock market?

A stock market is similar to a supermarket. A supermarket sells a variety of food, while a stock market sells a variety of stock. Stock is shares in a company. When you buy shares in a company you are buying part ownership of the company. You don't visit the stock exchange to buy or sell stock. Instead, you pay a stockbroker to buy and sell shares for you.

## A bull market

Imagine you buy 10 shares in Joe's Toy Company at $10 each. The company makes a very popular toy that lots of children buy. They make a profit and pay all their shareholders part of the profit (a dividend). Now lots of people want shares in Joe's Toy Company. The share price rises to $15 a share. If you sell your shares now you have made a profit of $50.

When lots of people want to buy new shares, and share prices rise, it is called a bull market.

A bull market

## A bear market

Imagine if Joe's Toy Company spent a lot of money developing a toy that was not popular. They didn't make a profit and there was no dividend paid to shareholders. No one wants to buy shares in the company, and the share price drops to $8 a share. If you sell your shares now you have made a loss of $20. When lots of people want to sell shares, and share prices fall, it is called a bear market.

A bear market

## Why sell shares in your company?

Joe owns Joe's Toy Company. He needs extra money to pay some toy designers to design new toys. Instead of borrowing money from the bank, Joe lists his company on the stock market. Some people think that Joe's Toy Company is a good business and so they buy shares. Joe gets the money from the shares to pay the toy designers.

## Why buy shares in a company?

When you have spare money you can invest it to try to make more money. One way to invest your money is to buy shares. If you invest in a company that does well, you will be paid a share of the company's profits (a dividend). Your shares will also increase in value, so that if you sell them, you make more profit. Of course, if the company you invest in does not make a profit you might lose money.

## Why do we need a stock market?

Joe could advertise his business for sale on the Internet, but what if it was too expensive for one person to buy? If Joe lists his company on the stock exchange, many people will each buy a small share in his company. Thousands of companies like Joe's sell their shares at the stock market, and millions of people buy (and sell) shares through the share market. The price of the shares is shown on a 'ticker board'. Stockbrokers watch the ticker board closely. They buy when the price is low, and sell when the price is high.

# IOU

## What are bonds?

A bond is an IOU. Mike's Machine Company needs money for a big project, but the bank cannot lend it that much money. Mike chooses to raise money by selling bond certificates. Mike's Machine Company sells the IOUs (the bond certificates), therefore the company is known as the **issuer**, while the buyer is the investor. As well as repaying the loan, the bond issuer is required to pay the investor interest payments for use of their money.

A bond certificate is an IOU

## How do bonds work?

Bonds are fixed-income securities because you get a fixed amount of money (income) if you keep them until maturity (end date). You might buy a bond certificate for $10,000, with an interest rate of 8 per cent, and a maturity of 10 years. Most interest payments are made every six months, so you'd receive two payments of $400 a year, for 10 years. When the bond reaches maturity, you would get your $10,000 back.

## Bonds or stock?

The difference between bonds and stocks is that when you buy stock you are buying a share in a company, but when you buy bonds you are lending money to a company. The benefit of shares is that you can vote at shareholder meetings and you share in the company profits (through dividends). If the company does really well you get a big profit. However, if the company does badly, you can lose money. The benefit of bonds is that if the company does badly it still has to pay you back the amount you lent it, plus the interest.

# Why bother with bonds?

Bonds carry less risk than shares, but also less profit. If you can't afford the risk of losing your money, then you should buy bonds. People who have retired can't afford to lose their money because they are living on 'fixed incomes' (they are not earning money any more). Retirees need to know how much interest they will receive every year, so that they can **budget** for their expenses. If you invest in bonds you know how much interest you will receive.

Bond investors budgeting

A 1918 war bonds poster

# Three types of bonds

Three types of bonds are government bonds, municipal bonds and corporate bonds.

When you buy government bonds you are lending money to your government. Bonds from stable governments, such as the United States, are considered extremely safe investments.

Municipal bonds are issued by states, cities, counties and districts. They finance hospitals, schools and airports.

Corporate bonds are issued by businesses to help them pay expenses. While corporate bonds are a higher risk than government bonds, they can earn a lot more money.

During World War II the United States government sold 'War Bonds' to raise money to pay for the war.

# Are these bonds AAA?

While bonds are safer than shares, they aren't risk-free. If the company goes **bankrupt**, the investor might lose some of the money they loaned. Credit rating agencies, such as Standard & Poor's, give grades to bonds based on their ability to pay a bond's principal and interest. Bonds are rated using letters ranging from 'AAA', which is the highest grade, to 'C' ('junk'), which is the lowest grade. Government bonds are the safest, because it is highly unlikely the government will go bankrupt.

# GLOBAL trade

## Globalisation

Have you ever looked at a globe? A globe is a ball that represents the Earth and shows all the countries of the world. Globalisation means the worldwide (or global) spread of goods, services or ideas. When something is used in many countries around the world, it is said to have become global. The global financial system refers to financial institutions such as banks, which trade on a worldwide, rather than a national, level.

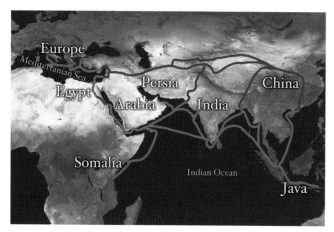

A map showing the ancient silk routes

## The silk routes

Globalisation is not a new idea. In ancient times the important civilisations of China, India, Egypt, Persia, Arabia and Italy traded with each other. There were trade routes connecting all these countries. The major trade item from China was silk, which was sent overland to many other countries. These ancient routes are now known as the silk routes. Traders, merchants, pilgrims and soldiers travelled along these routes. They transported goods such as silk, perfume, spices, medicines, jewels, glassware and food from one country to another. In the late Middle Ages, trade over the silk routes declined as sea trade increased.

## Free trade

Are all the food, toys and clothes you buy made in the country where you live? Most countries import some goods, as it's often cheaper to import items than to make them.

To get extra money countries usually charge an import tax on items that are imported. Sometimes one country will agree with another country to remove the import taxes they charge each other. This makes the items cheaper for consumers to buy, so both countries sell more of their product to each other. This is called a free trade agreement.

These clothes may have been made in another country

Coffee beans being sorted and pulped

## The big three

After World War II ended, people throughout the world wanted to prevent another war by encouraging countries to cooperate in trade and finance. Meetings were held and some international organisations were set up. There are currently three global organisations that control international finance and trade. They are the International Monetary Fund, the World Bank and the World Trade Organization. The International Monetary Fund helps countries solve money and trade issues. The World Bank provides funding for projects in developing countries. The World Trade Organization deals with any arguments between trading countries.

## Trade alliances

Throughout the world, countries form alliances with their neighbours so that they can trade with them. The largest trading alliance in Europe is the European Economic Area (EEA). It has 28 member countries, which allow the free movement of goods, persons, services and capital between the EEA countries.

The Asia-Pacific Economic Cooperation (APEC) has 21 member countries, whose inhabitants represent 40.5 per cent of the world's population. APEC trades and invests in the Asia-Pacific region.

In North America, the Free Trade Agreement, (NAFTA) links Canada, the United States and Mexico. In South America, the 12 member Community of Nations (SACN) is working towards becoming a continent-wide free trade zone with a single currency and a single passport.

Some brands are known globally

## Brands across the world

Some brands of goods are totally global. This means that their business is operating not just in one city, or one country, but in many countries throughout the world. These companies are very successful because they have a huge number of customers around the world. No matter where in the world you are, there are certain products that are familiar to everyone. You are never far from a familiar hamburger, soft drink or car.

# THE EURO
## takes over

### The European Union

The European Union currently has 27 member countries. These member countries include Austria, Belgium, Bulgaria, Cyprus, Czech Republic, Denmark, Estonia, Finland, France, Germany, Greece, Hungary, Ireland, Italy, Latvia, Lithuania, Luxembourg, Malta, the Netherlands, Poland, Portugal, Romania, Slovakia, Slovenia, Spain, Sweden and the United Kingdom. These countries have agreed to a single system of laws and trade.

### Euro coins

The Euro is divided into 100 Euro-cents. The coin denominations are 1c, 2c, 5c, 10c, 20c, 50c, €1, €2. In order to avoid using the two smallest coins, bills in some countries, e.g. the Netherlands, are rounded to the nearest five cents.

The **obverse** side of the coins shows the value, and a map of Europe. The **reverse** side shows an image chosen by the country that issued the coin. Euro coins from any country may be used in any other country in the Eurozone.

### The Euro sign

Although the Euro has been in use since 2002, it only became the official currency of the European Union on 1 December 2009. The Euro currency sign is a capital E with 2 horizontal lines running through it. The € symbol represents both the Greek epsilon, and the first letter of the word Europe. The two parallel lines represent the stability of the Euro. The international three-letter code for the Euro is EUR.

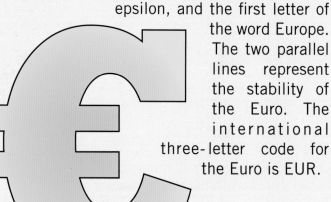

# Euro banknotes

Euro notes are issued in €500, €200, €100, €50, €20, €10 and €5. Euro notes have common designs on both sides. Each banknote has its own colour. The front of each note features windows or gateways while the back has bridges. Some of the highest denominations, such as the €500, are not issued in all countries, though they remain legal tender throughout the Eurozone.

# The Eurozone

The Euro is currently the sole currency of 16 EU countries: Austria, Belgium, Cyprus, Finland, France, Germany, Greece, Ireland, Italy, Luxembourg, Malta, the Netherlands, Portugal, Slovakia, Slovenia and Spain. These countries are called the 'Eurozone', an area that contains 326 million people, and is the second largest economy in the world. Other countries (especially in Africa) accept the Euro alongside their own currency, making the Euro the second most traded currency in the world after the US dollar.

# The € or the £?

Most countries in the European Union have adopted the Euro as their currency. The French franc, Italian lira and Austrian schilling have all been replaced by the Euro. However, some countries continue to use their own currencies. The currency in Denmark is the krone, and in the United Kingdom is the pound. In the future these countries might replace their currencies with the Euro. In Denmark prices are sometimes shown in both kroner and euros.

# The right PRICE

## What is the right price?

Have your parents or grandparents ever told you that things used to cost less than they do now? Why do things cost more now? Who decides the price for food or cars or toys? If you buy a trolley of groceries today, will you still be able to buy an identical trolley full for the same price in two years' time? If you pay more in two years' time then there has been some inflation. If you pay less, then there has been deflation. If the groceries cost the same in two years' time there has been price stability.

Will the price of these groceries have changed in two years' time?

## Inflation

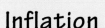

Inflation is an increase in the prices of goods and services over time. This means money is worth less because you can buy less for your money. Inflation occurs when the demand for goods and services exceeds the supply. During a rainy winter there is a high demand for umbrellas. The umbrella factory tries to keep up with the demand by getting the staff to work longer hours. The factory boss then has to pay the staff more money. To get that money he has to increase the price of umbrellas. The people can't afford to buy umbrellas because the price has increased.

## Deflation

Deflation is the opposite of inflation. The price of goods and services falls over time.

During a dry winter no one buys umbrellas. The umbrella factory cuts back on production by getting the staff to work shorter hours. The boss is forced to reduce the price of umbrellas in the hope that he will sell some, but no one wants to buy them. Because the boss has less money and the staff are working shorter hours they get paid less. The staff can't afford to buy things because they have less money.

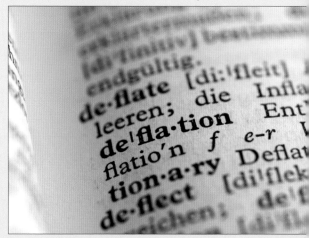

When supply is greater than demand the price goes down, but wages also go down

## Price stability

Price stability means that the price of goods and services stays the same over time. It is defined as keeping inflation at about 2 per cent. Most countries use a CPI (Consumer Price Index) to measure the price of goods and services. The CPI tracks the price people pay for food, education, clothing, housing, transport, health and even recreation. The **Reserve Bank** tries to keep any price changes between one and three per cent. If the CPI rises or falls by more than this then the Reserve Bank adjusts short-term interest rates. Increasing interest rates reduces domestic spending by making money more expensive. Decreasing interest rates makes money cheaper and increases or stimulates domestic spending. It's like driving a car. To keep at a same speed over a hilly road, you sometimes use your brake and you sometimes use your accelerator.

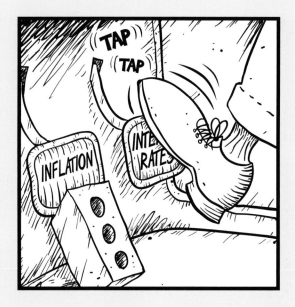

In times of price stability there is high employment

## Why *do we need price stability?*

When prices are stable, people and businesses are more confident. They can plan for the future without worrying about whether they should be spending or saving money. Price stability means businesses can accurately work out how many staff they need, which leads to high employment. High employment means more people are earning and spending a wage. When people are able to spend more money, more goods need to be made. This means more people need to be employed. So price stability improves the whole economy.

## The European Central Bank

The European Central Bank, and the central bank of each country in the Eurozone, work together to maintain price stability in the Euro area. More than 300 million people in 16 countries use the Euro as their currency. They depend on the European Central Bank to maintain price stability within the Eurozone.

The European Central Bank in Frankfurt

# BLACK DAYS

## Black Monday and Black Tuesday

In the late 1920s, America was prosperous and people borrowed money to invest in the share market. They thought that share prices would keep rising and they would get rich. However, on Thursday October 24, 1929 share prices stopped rising. A few people quickly sold their shares. This caused share prices to drop on Friday. On Monday, everyone rushed to sell their shares as soon as the stock market opened, causing share prices to crash. On Tuesday, share prices dropped even further. This became known as the Wall Street Crash of 1929. The two days when prices crashed are called Black Monday and Black Tuesday.

## The Great Depression

After the Wall Street Crash people were left with no money, no jobs and no homes. It was the beginning of the Great Depression in America. The Great Depression quickly spread to almost every country in the world. Wages, taxes, profits and prices dropped. Unemployment in the United States rose to 25 per cent. Crop prices fell by 60 per cent as no one had any money to spend. It was a time of much hardship and it didn't end until World War II.

In a depression everyone faces hard times

## Not again!

There has not been another Great Depression since the 1930s; however, there has been another Black Monday and Black Tuesday stock market crash. On Monday, October 19, 1987, stock markets around the world crashed. The crash began in Hong Kong, then spread to Europe and the United States. The Black Monday decline was the largest one-day percentage decline in stock market history. In Australia and New Zealand the 1987 crash is referred to as Black Tuesday because of the time zone difference.

## A recent recession

The USA entered a recession at the end of 2007. This was partly caused by a drop in house prices. People who bought houses when prices were high were left with a mortgage that was higher than the value of their house. In 2008 people stopped buying non-essential goods. Because businesses couldn't sell their goods they had to lay off staff. In 2008, 2.6 million US jobs were eliminated. Other countries such as the UK, Canada, India, Japan and China were affected by the US recession. However, Australia avoided a recession in 2009, and had positive growth against the overall global economic downturn.

## Recessions

A recession is a slowdown in the economy. Personal income and business profit drop, there are more bankruptcies and higher unemployment. Recessions happen when the economy is unstable, such as in times of war, energy crises or currency crises.

The average recession lasts about a year. Governments try to control recessions by increasing government spending and decreasing taxation, so that there is less unemployment and people spend more money.

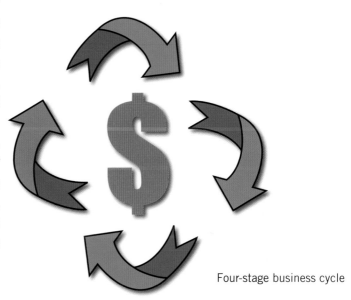

Four-stage business cycle

## Economic cycle

Some people believe that economic growth and recessions happen in cycles that repeat about every 10 years. The economic cycle has four stages:
1. Expansion. There is an increase in production and prices, and low interest rates.
2. Crisis. The stock exchanges crash and many businesses go bankrupt.
3. Recession. Prices drop, there is less production, and interest rates are high.
4. Recovery. The stock market recovers because of the fall in prices and incomes.

Unemployed workers job searching in an economic recession

# Currency around

# THE WORLD

## Asia

Asia is the largest continent in the world, and it is rich in natural resources such as metals. There are nearly 50 countries, from Russia in the north to Indonesia in the south. Each country has its own currency. Some currencies are well known, such as the Indian rupee, the Thai baht, the Japanese yen and the Russian rouble. Other currencies, such as the Macau pataka, the Kazakhstan tenge, and the Laos kip are less well known.

A five-rupee note

A 500-franc note from the Central African Republic

## Africa

Many African countries change their currency when a new government takes power, but the value of the notes remains the same. Street sellers will illegally exchange local currency for US dollars (which are valuable because they aren't affected by local inflation). In rural areas people barter because the items being exchanged are more valuable than the local currency. You can eat a chicken but not a banknote. The African Union wants to introduce a single currency, the Afro, for the entire continent by 2023. This will do away with more than 50 currencies, including the dalasi, the loti, the ouguiya, and the metical.

## Oceania

Australia, New Zealand and the Pacific Islands make up the diverse area named Oceania. Australia and New Zealand are the two strongest economies, while the small island nations rely on either tourism or foreign aid for income. The Australian dollar, the New Zealand dollar, the US dollar, and the Pacific franc are the main currencies. Samoa, Papua New Guinea, Vanuatu and Tonga have their own currencies.

Vanuatuan vatu coins

Swedish kronor

## Europe

There are 27 countries in the European Union. In 2010 the Euro was being used by 16 countries as their official currency, and eight other countries were preparing to accept the Euro as their currency. Three countries in the European Union have permission to keep using their own currencies. They are the United Kingdom, Denmark and Sweden.

## North America

The three countries in North America—Canada, the US and Mexico—each have their own currencies. They are the Canadian dollar, the US dollar and the Mexican peso. It has been suggested that these three countries give up their currencies and use a new North American currency called the Amero. However, many people oppose this. The US dollar is the most stable currency in the world, and if it were changed to an Amero it might become less stable.

A US one-dollar note

## South America

There are 13 currencies in South America. Argentina, Chile, Colombia and Uruguay each use their own peso. Ecuador uses the US dollar, and French Guiana the Euro. The remaining countries have their own currencies. In Peru, there is a dance where the dancers wear a square flat hat called an aqarapi, which has antique coins hanging from its borders.

Peruvian dancer wearing a traditional hat decorated with coins

# Fascinating FACTS

## Traditions

There are traditions throughout the world concerning money. In England, small silver coins are hidden in the Christmas pudding. At weddings in Greece and Poland, male guests give money to the bride to buy a dance from her. The newlywed couple get to keep the money. In China at New Year, children receive a red envelope containing money, from their parents.

## The £ sign

The '£' sign developed over the years from the letter 'L', the initial letter of the Latin word '*libra*', meaning a pound of money. It is generally agreed that the letters 's' for shilling and 'd' for penny stand for the Latin words '*solidus*' and '*denarius*' respectively. These were originally Roman coins of considerably greater value than the shilling and the penny.

## Maundy Money

Maundy Thursday is the Thursday before Easter. On this day in the UK, the Queen distributes Maundy Money to chosen elderly people. At the ceremony the Queen hands each person two small leather string purses. One, a red purse, contains ordinary money; the other, a white purse, contains silver Maundy coins consisting of the same number of pence as the years of the sovereign's age.

Queen Elizabeth II

# The $ sign

The origin of the '$' sign can be traced back to the reverse design of the Spanish Eight Reales. This coin was widely used by many countries during the late 18th and 19th centuries. The reverse design of the Eight Reales shows two columns with an intertwining ribbon, which are also known as 'Pillars of Hercules with a snake'. It is this design and the fact that the coin was often known as the 'Spanish dollar', that is thought to have inspired the familiar $ symbol.

# Holey Dollar and Dump

In the 1800s, two settlements in Australia (Prince Edward Island and New South Wales) grew in population very quickly, and they ran out of coins. Governor Macquarie decided the cheapest way to make new coins was to punch holes in Spanish dollars to create two new coins. The larger coin was named the 'Holey Dollar' and the smaller coin was named a 'Dump'. The governor had 40,000 Spanish Eight Reales made into holey dollars and dumps. The Holey Dollar and Dump have now been demonetised. This means they are no longer 'legal tender'. They are the only Australian coins which have had their 'legal tender' status removed.

# What happens to old money?

Money does not last forever. Coins and banknotes get worn and damaged. Coins are melted down and the metal reused to make new coins. Paper money can't be reused so it is destroyed. Every year the US Treasury destroys damaged currency valued at over $30 million. At the Treasury, experts examine the damaged coins and notes. They will pay the bearer the value of the currency before they destroy it.

Burning an old 500-franc note

# MANAGING your money

## Earning money

There are thousands of ways for teenagers to earn money. Look at your skills and decide what would interest you. A tennis player could become a coach for younger children. A musician could get a job at a rest home or mall. There are many non-skilled jobs including cleaning cars, delivering leaflets, growing produce to sell or working at a supermarket. Sophie works as a lifeguard on the weekends. She earns $150 a week.

Sophie at work

## Spending money

Sophie needs to pay her mobile phone bill of $40 per month, and her bus fare of $64 a month. She spends $80 a month on lunches. In one month Sophie spends $120 buying a CD, a magazine, some makeup, and going to the movies. How much money does Sophie have left at the end of the month?

A bought lunch

## Saving money

Saving money is important, because if you don't save some of your earnings you'll never be able to afford expensive items, such as your own car. You also need savings in case you lose your job.

Sophie wants to buy a car. When Sophie finds out how much a car costs, she realises that it will take her years to earn enough money. Sophie offers to work more hours, she bikes to work, and she takes homemade lunches. Now that she has a goal, Sophie spends less of her money on things such as magazines.

# Need it or want it?

You have a part-time job and you are earning money. What will you do with it? It's your decision. Will you save it, spend it, or invest it? Start by writing a list of needs and wants. Make sure that you have enough money to pay for your needs, before you spend money on wants.

Planning how to spend your money is called budgeting. Budget so that you always have some money left at the end of the month to put into a savings account.

Budgeting pocket money

# Spend less

Earning money is hard work, so don't waste your money. If you must buy magazines, rent them to your friends to read so that you get back some of the cost of buying them. Use the library instead of always buying new books. Buy clothes and toys secondhand. Sell toys and games you no longer want. Don't **impulse buy** at the mall. Make a list of what you need to **purchase** and how much it will cost. Put your savings in a bank account so you're not tempted to spend it on things you don't need. Try to save more money this month than you did last month. You'll be amazed at how quickly your savings grow.

Raj studying

# Investing money

Raj wants to become a vet. He is already saving for his university costs. Raj works as a maths tutor after school, and he earns $300 a week. Raj invests most of his money into a bank savings scheme, where he is paid 6 per cent interest. Every six months he withdraws a lump sum and puts it into a three-year term deposit where he receives 8 per cent interest. By investing his money instead of spending it, Raj is making his money grow.

Garage sales are great places to buy things second hand, or to sell things you no longer need

# ACTIVITIES

## Design a banknote

Use the information on page 12 to help you design your own money. Start with the size, shape and colour of your banknote. Each banknote needs a background, a picture, the value, country of issue, hologram, metal strip and serial number. Print your banknote and use it to pay family and friends when you owe an IOU, or use it in a Monopoly-type game.

## Coin rubbing

Choose a coin with an interesting design on it. Place the coin under a piece of paper. Hold the coin by the edges. Keeping the coin still (hold it or tape it down), rub over its surface with the side of a crayon. The outline of the coin will appear on your paper.

You can make a coin rubbing collection or you could make gift cards with coin rubbings on them.

## Milk carton moneybox

Wash out a milk carton. Decorate the milk carton by painting or gluing paper on it. Cut a slot in the side. Put all your spare change in your moneybox. Once the moneybox is full, open it and decide whether you want to spend or bank the money.

## Design a coin

Nine-year-old Florence Jackson, from Bristol, is the first child ever to work with the Royal Mint to design a UK coin. Florence won the opportunity to design a coin celebrating the Olympics in London in 2012. She entered a competition on the TV program *Blue Peter*. Florence's design was chosen from 17,000 entries.

# Currencies around the world

Make a list of currencies around the world. There are approximately 180 legal tender currencies in use throughout the world. If you make your list alphabetical by country, start with the Afghan afghani and finish with the Zimbabwean dollar. How many did you get in between? If you make your list alphabetical by currency start with the afghani and finish with the złoty. Don't forget to include the following currencies: cedi, dalasi, loti, ouguiya, tala, hryvnia and quetzal.

# Sayings about money

Find the meanings for the following sayings. Do you agree with them?
- Safe as Fort Knox
- Nest egg
- Stretching the dollar
- Safe as the Bank of England
- Money makes the world go around
- Money on hand
- Money doesn't bring happiness
- Time is money
- Money doesn't grow on trees
- Worth their salt
- The hobby of kings

# Vanishing coin

A fun way to earn a little pocket money is to learn a coin trick. If people want to see the trick they have to supply the coin. If you make the coin disappear, your audience will usually let you keep it. There is more than one vanishing coin trick. This is an easy one.

You need:
A large piece and a small piece of identically coloured paper
A drinking glass
A cloth
A wand

Preparation
Trace the rim of the glass onto the small piece of paper. Cut out the circle of paper and glue it to the rim.

Performance
Show the audience the coin. Place it on the large piece of paper. Cover the glass with the cloth. Move the glass on top of the coin. Tap the glass. Say some magic words, then pull the cloth off the glass. The coin will have disappeared.

Secret
The paper on the rim of the glass covers the coin so it appears that the coin has disappeared.

# GLOSSARY

**Bankrupt.** Legally declared to be unable to pay off personal debts.

**Barter.** Trading without using money.

**Blank.** A round piece of metal that gets stamped with a die to turn it into a coin.

**Budget.** A plan showing how money will be spent and saved over a period of time.

**Cheque book.** A small printed form that instructs your bank to pay a person an amount from your bank account.

**Counterfeit.** A realistic copy of something, made in order to trick people.

**Credit card.** A card issued by a bank that allows someone to purchase goods but pay for them later.

**Currency.** A system of money used in a particular country.

**Debit card.** A card that allows you to pay for goods by automatic transfer of money out of your account.

**Deposit.** Money left in the care of the bank.

**Dies.** Metal designs that are stamped onto blanks turning them into coins.

**Double trade.** Trade with more than one person, so that everyone ends up with the item they want.

**Economy.** The goods and services provided to and used by a community.

**Electronic banking.** Doing banking transactions by using a computer instead of going to the bank.

**Electrum.** A natural mixture of gold and silver.

**Embossing.** Decorating the surface with slightly raised design.

**Expenditure.** An amount of money spent.

**Forgery.** An illegal copy of a document or painting that has been made to look genuine.

**Hologram.** A three-dimensional image.

**Impulse buy.** Buying something without planning or budgeting for it.

**Income.** Money received as payment..

**Inflation.** Higher prices for goods because there is increased demand or less available goods.

**Intaglio.** A security feature of slightly raised printing on a banknote.

**Interest.** A payment made for the use of money.

**Invest.** To use money to buy shares or bonds in the hope of making a profit.

**Legal tender.** Currency that can be legally used to pay for something.

**Mint.** A place where coins are made, or to stamp coins out of metal.

**Obverse.** The front of a coin. It usually has a head on it.

**Polymer.** A tough thin plastic used for banknote printing in some countries.

**Profit.** The money gained after costs have been paid for.

**Purchase.** Get something by paying money for it.

**Reserve Bank.** The central bank of a country, which is responsible for issuing currency.

**Reverse.** The back of a coin. It states the coin's value.

**Running cash note.** A handwritten receipt which promised to pay the person back on demand.

**Security thread.** A thread running through a banknote, which is hard for counterfeiters to copy.

**Serial numbers.** A set of identifying numbers marked on a banknote.

**Shadow image.** A darkened image behind the lighter image.

**Supply and demand.** Items are more in demand when their supply is limited.

**Symbolic value.** To give an item an agreed-upon value, so that it can be used for trade.

**Trading.** Swapping with someone, one item for a different item.

**Transaction.** A business deal between two people.

**Treasury.** The government finance department in charge of managing the country's money.

**Watermark.** A design hidden in paper, that can only be seen when the paper is held up to the light.

# Want to KNOW MORE?

Banknote Printing
United States Bureau of Engraving and Printing http://www.newmoney.gov/newmoney/learning/download.htm

Bank of England.
http://www.bankofengland.co.uk

Coin Printing
The Australian Mint www.ramint.gov.au (try Frequently Asked Questions, or the museum).
The United States Mint. http:www.usmint.gov/kids/ (fun games, history and news)

Design a Banknote
http://www.worldofmoney.birminghamblackhistory.com/currency/paper2.html

Euro. The official European Central Bank website
http://www.euro.ecb.int

Finding Forgeries
Australian Currency
http://www.rba.gov.au/CurrencyNotes/SecurityFeaturesAndCounterfeitDetection/counterfeit_detection_guide.html
USA Currency
http://www.newmoney.gov/newmoney/

Florence Jackson's winning coin design
http://www.royalmint.com/olympicgames/BluePeterCoinDesign.aspx

Magic Coin Tricks
http://learncoinmagictricks.com/

Numisnet World
www.vision.net.au

Money Guide
www.sorted.org.nz

Money Museum
http://www.moneymuseum.com

Tasmanian Numismatic Society (which has interesting online newsletters).
http://www.vision.net.au/~pwood/tns.html

UK Treasury
http://www.treasury.gov.uk

US Mint
www.usmint.gov/kids/games

# INDEX

First published in 2011 by Young Reed, an imprint of New Holland Publishers (Australia) Pty Ltd, Sydney • Auckland • London • Cape Town

www.newholland.com.au

1/66 Gibbes Street Chatswood NSW 2067 Australia, 218 Lake Road Northcote Auckland New Zealand, 86 Edgware Road London W2 2EA United Kingdom, 80 McKenzie Street Cape Town 8001 South Africa

National Library of Australia Cataloguing-in-Publication Data:
Ellis, Julie. Currencies of the world / Julie Ellis.

ISBN: 9781921580031 (hbk.)

Includes bibliographical references and index. Money--Juvenile literature.

332.4

Publisher: Diane Jardine, Publishing manager: Lliane Clarke, Project editor: Talina McKenzie, Proofreader: Victoria Fisher, Designer: Amanda Tarlau, Cover design: Celeste Vlok, Production manager: Olga Dementiev, Printer: Toppan Leefung Printing Limited (China)

Image credits: pp8 (Cacao beans) David Monniaux, pp9 (Yap money stones) Eric Guinther, pp9 (Gold nugget) Rob Lawinsky, pp10 (Athenian coins) PHGCOM, pp12 (All) Royal Australian Mint, pp18, (Al Khazneh) R. Castino, pp20, (Potsini) Christophe Meneboeuf, pp27, (Speedboat toy) Kolling, pp31, (Sorting coffee beans) Roh Street Cafe, pp32, (European member states) Ssolbergj, pp34, (Umbrella) Jean D'Alembert, pp35 (European Central Bank) Eric Chan, pp38 (Swedish kronor) Martin Olsson, pp41 (Emblem of Charles I of Spain) Ignacio Gavira, pp41 (Holey dollar) Mike Peel, pp41 (Burning francs) TCY.